KIDS PROGRAMMING 2

Written by:
Kensho Koyama &
Mindaugas Ramanauskis

CHESTNUT TREE
LEARNING©

Written by: Kensho Koyama & Mindaugas Ramanauskis

INDEX

ATTENTION!!

Before using this textbook, please access all lesson materials using the link below

- Unit 1-10 Warm-ups
- Student lesson projects
- Teacher lesson projects (completed)

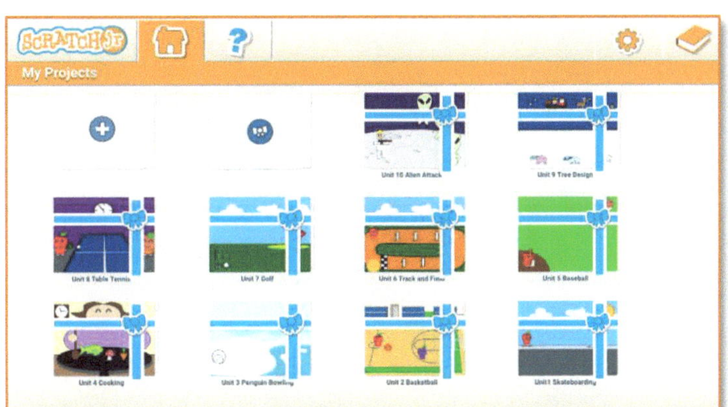

UNIT 1: Skateboarding

1.

skateboard

2.

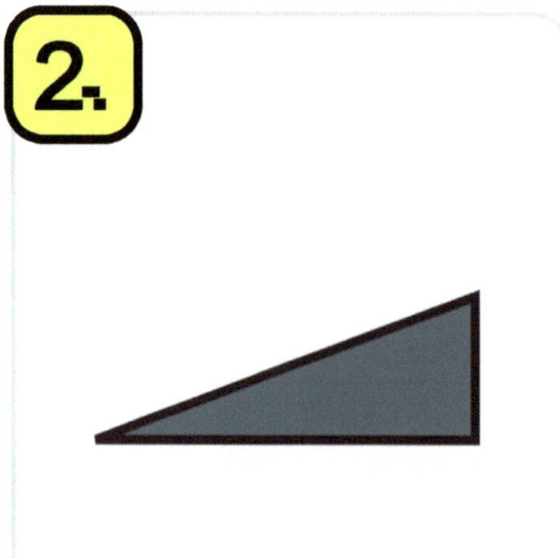

ramp

3.

street

Skateboarding Chant

Ride, ride my **skateboard**,
on the **street**,
do a **trick** on the **ramp**,
jump, you can do it, you re a champ

WORDBANK	
skateboard	skate
ramp	trick
street	ride

UNIT 1: Skateboarding

1.

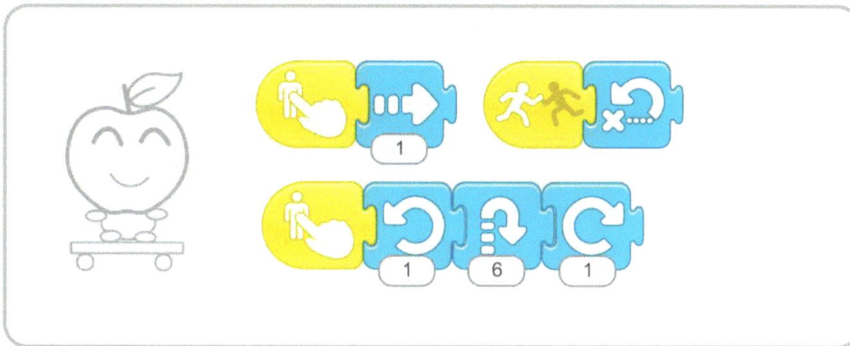

Yes I did it!

2.

Yes I did it!

3.

Yes I did it!

Extra Programming

UNIT 1: Skateboarding

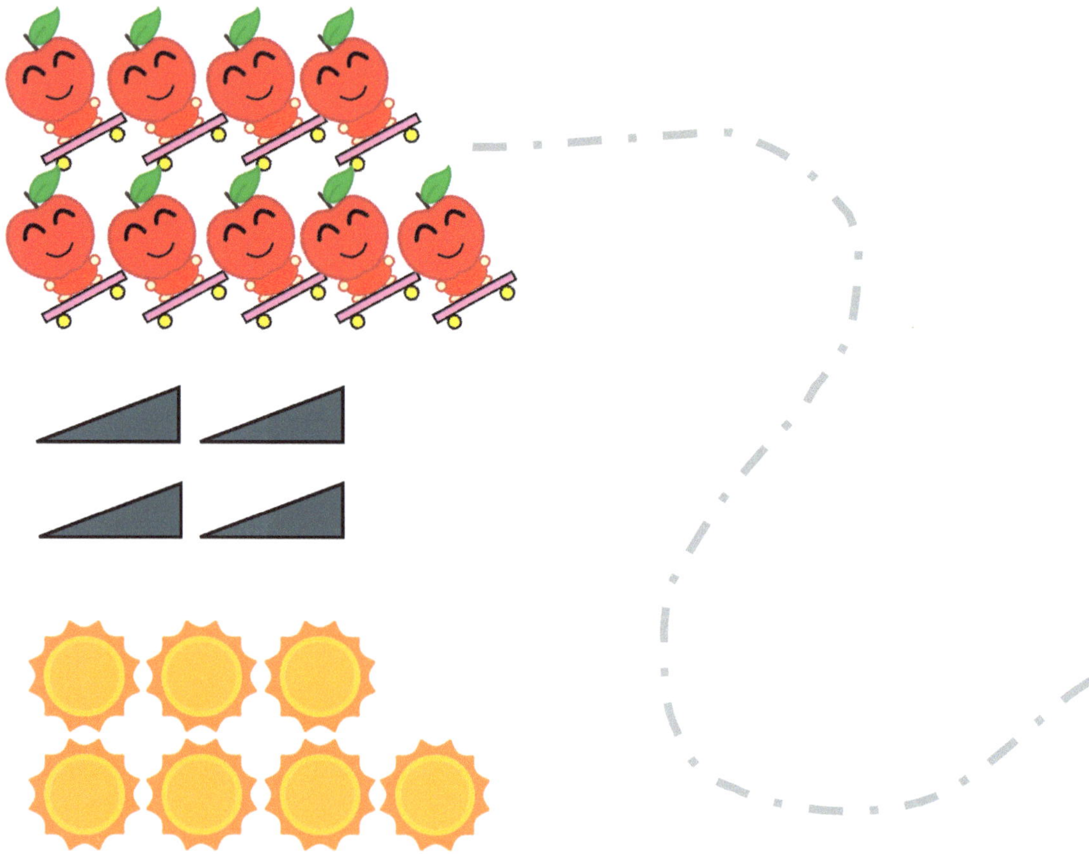

4

7

9

Color:

UNIT 1: Skateboarding

Code Search:

Maze:

UNIT 2: Basketball

1.

basketball

2.

court

3.

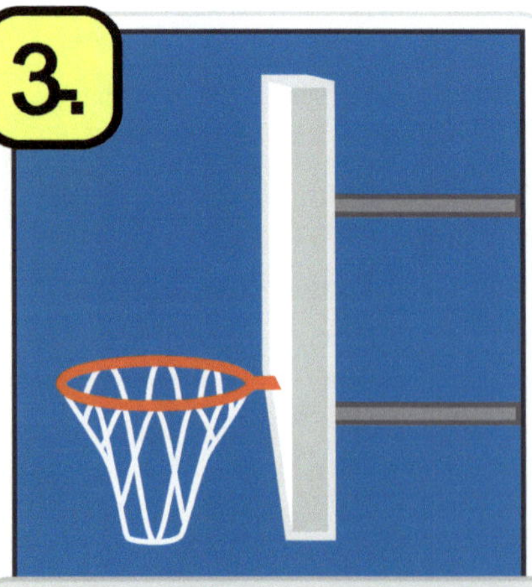

hoop

Basketball Chant

Bounce, **bounce**, the **basketball**

On the **court play basketball**

Dunk the ball in the **hoop**

How many times can you shoot?

WORDBANK	
basketball	bounce
court	play
hoop	dunk

Can you play basketball?

UNIT 2: Basketball

1.

Yes I did it!

2.

Yes I did it!

3.

Yes I did it!

Extra Programming

Yes I did it!

UNIT 2: Basketball

Connect:

5

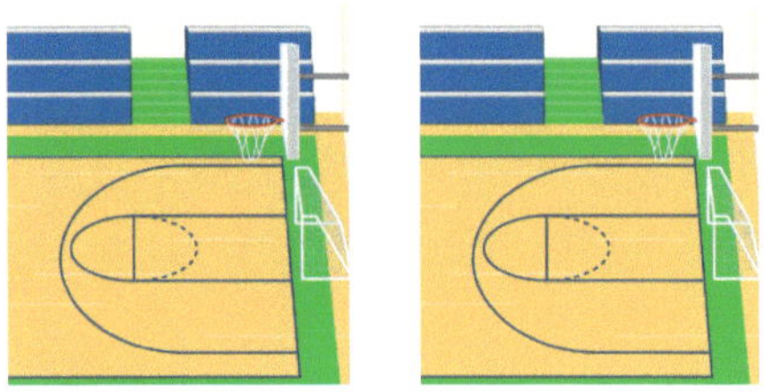

2

10

Count: 1 - 10

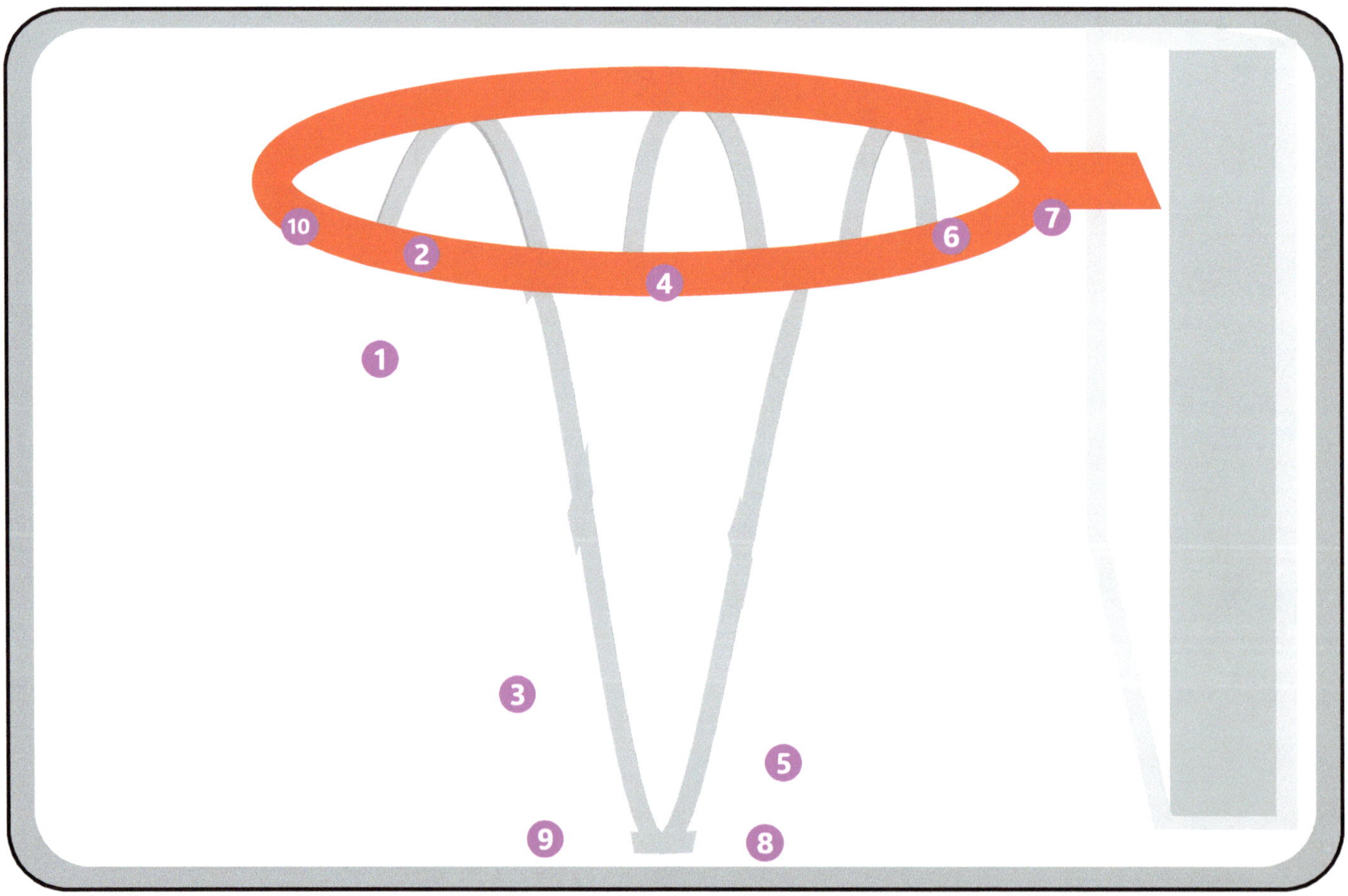

UNIT 2: Basketball

Maze:

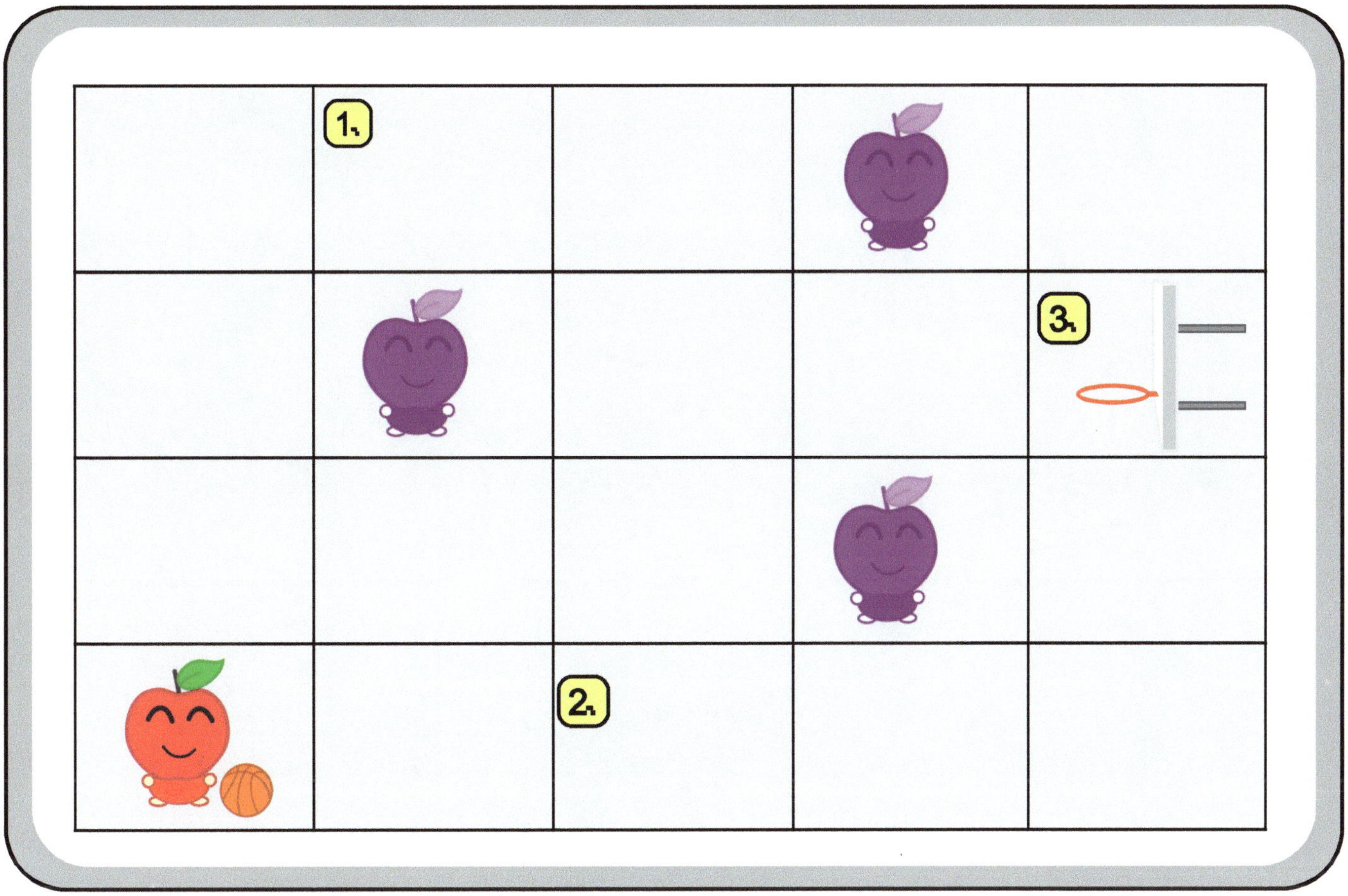

Maze code:

1.

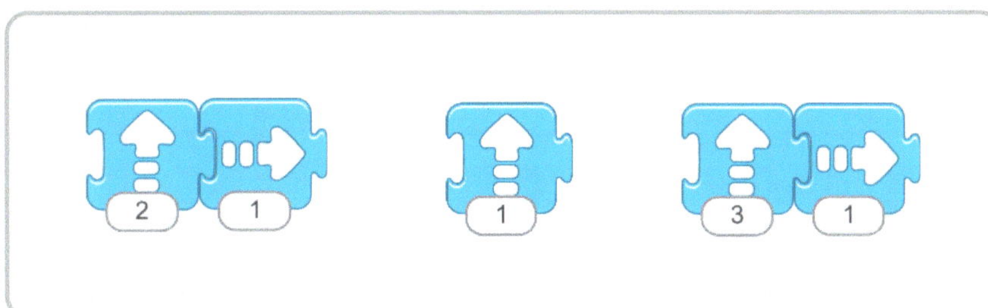

2.

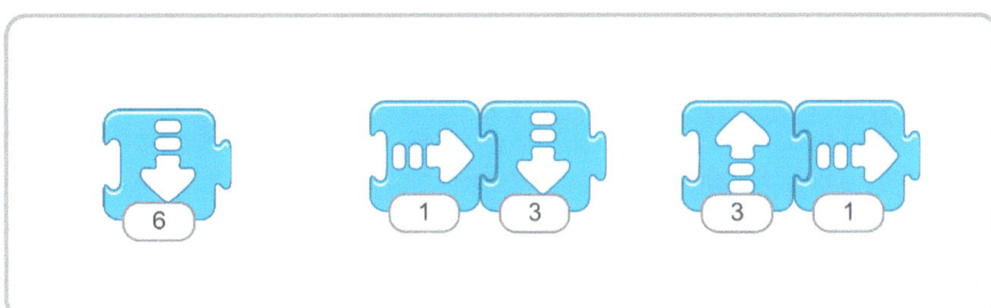

3.

UNIT 3: Penguin Bowling

1.

penguins

2.

snowman

3.

ice

Penguin Chant

Penguin bowling (2x), let's go **penguin** ♫
bowing, make a **snowman** head and **roll**
it at the **penguins**, **hit** them all, strike!
penguins fall off the **ice**!!

WORDBANK	
penguins	hit
snowman	roll
ice	fall

UNIT 3: Penguin Bowling

1.

Yes I did it!

2.

Yes I did it!

3.

Yes I did it!

Extra Programming

Yes I did it!

UNIT 3: Penguin Bowling

Connect:

3

8

9

Find the code:

UNIT 3: Penguin Bowling

Maze:

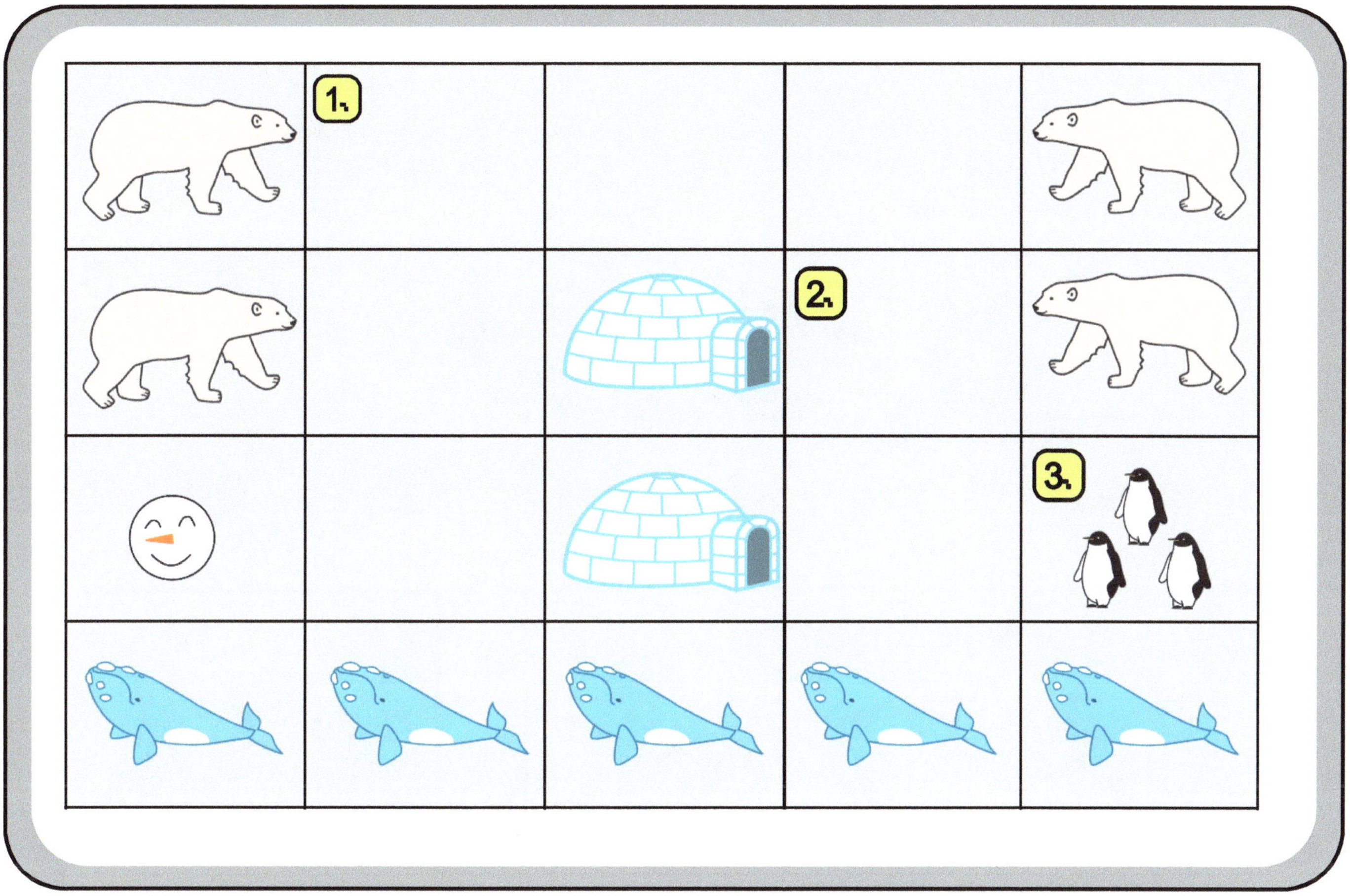

Maze code:

1.

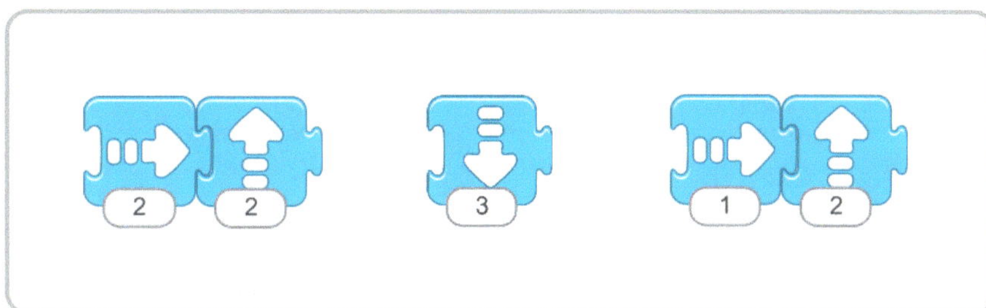

2.

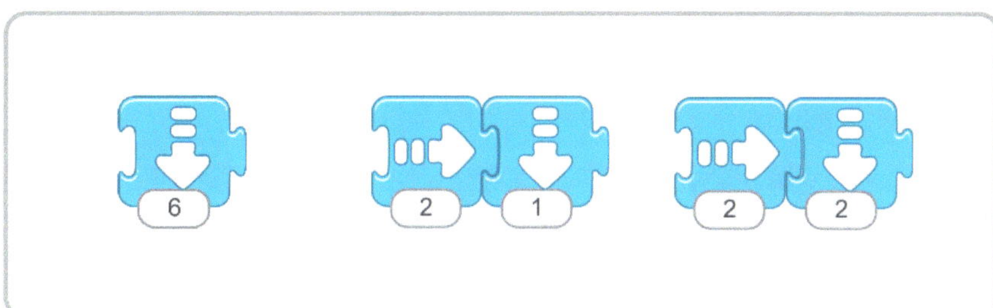

3.

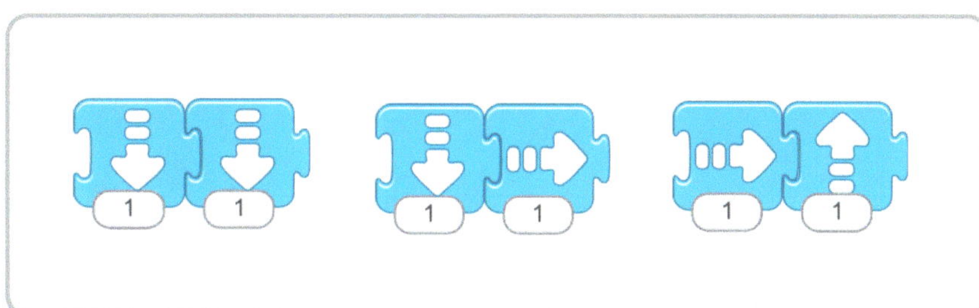

UNIT 4: Cooking

1.

spoon

2.

frypan

3.

dish

Cooking Chant

I'm **cooking**, **cooking** all the food,
I'm in the kitchen, **cooking** for me and you,
stir in the **frypan** with my **spoon**,
make a **dish**, for me an you

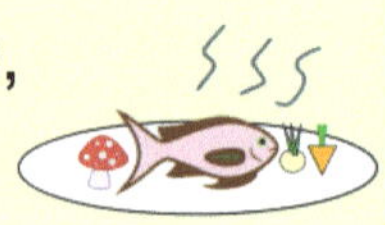

WORDBANK	
spoon	stir
pan	cooking
dish	make

UNIT 4: Cooking

1.

Yes I did it!

2.

Yes I did it!

3.

Yes I did it!

Extra Programming

Yes I did it!

UNIT 4: Cooking

Connect:

6

4

2

Color and Complete:

Cook the food

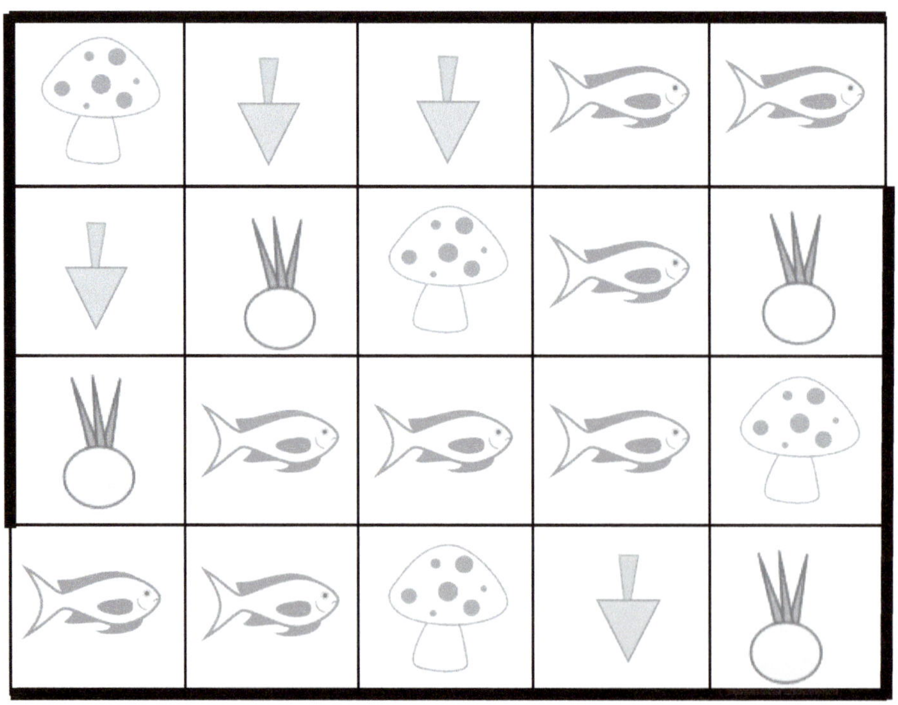

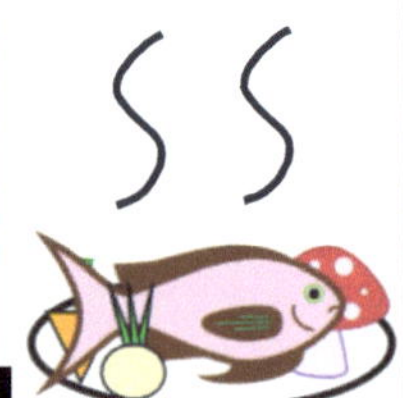

UNIT 4: Cooking

Write:

1 1 1 1

2 2 2

3 3 3

4 4 4

5 5 5

Color:

UNIT 5: Baseball

1.

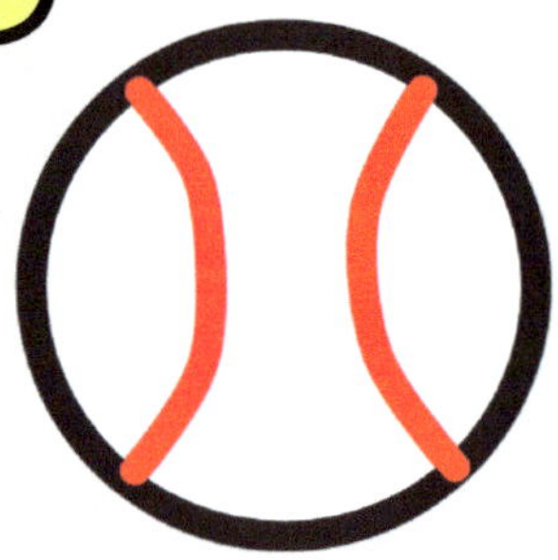

baseball

2.

batter

3.

glove

Baseball Chant

Oh, oh, the **baseball** game, the good fun
baseball game, **swing, swing** the **baseball**
bat, the **baseball** is coming fast, ♫
hit, hit, the **baseball** run before they **catch**

WORDBANK	
baseball	catch
bat	hit
batter	swing

UNIT 5: Baseball

1.

Yes I did it!

2.

Yes I did it!

3.

Yes I did it!

Extra Programming

Yes I did it!

UNIT 5: Baseball

Connect:

3

5

8

Maze:

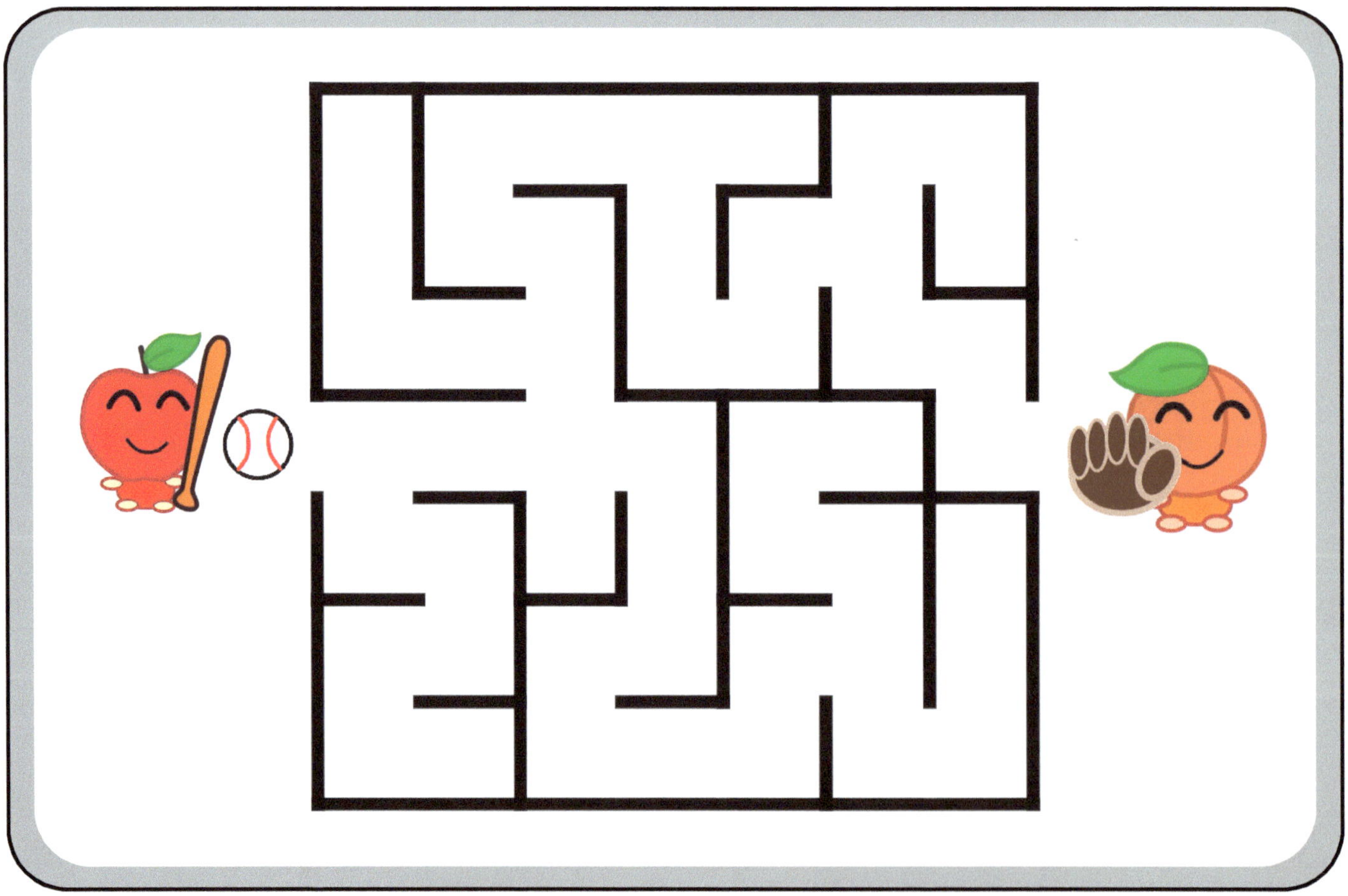

UNIT 5: Baseball

Code Search:

Color:

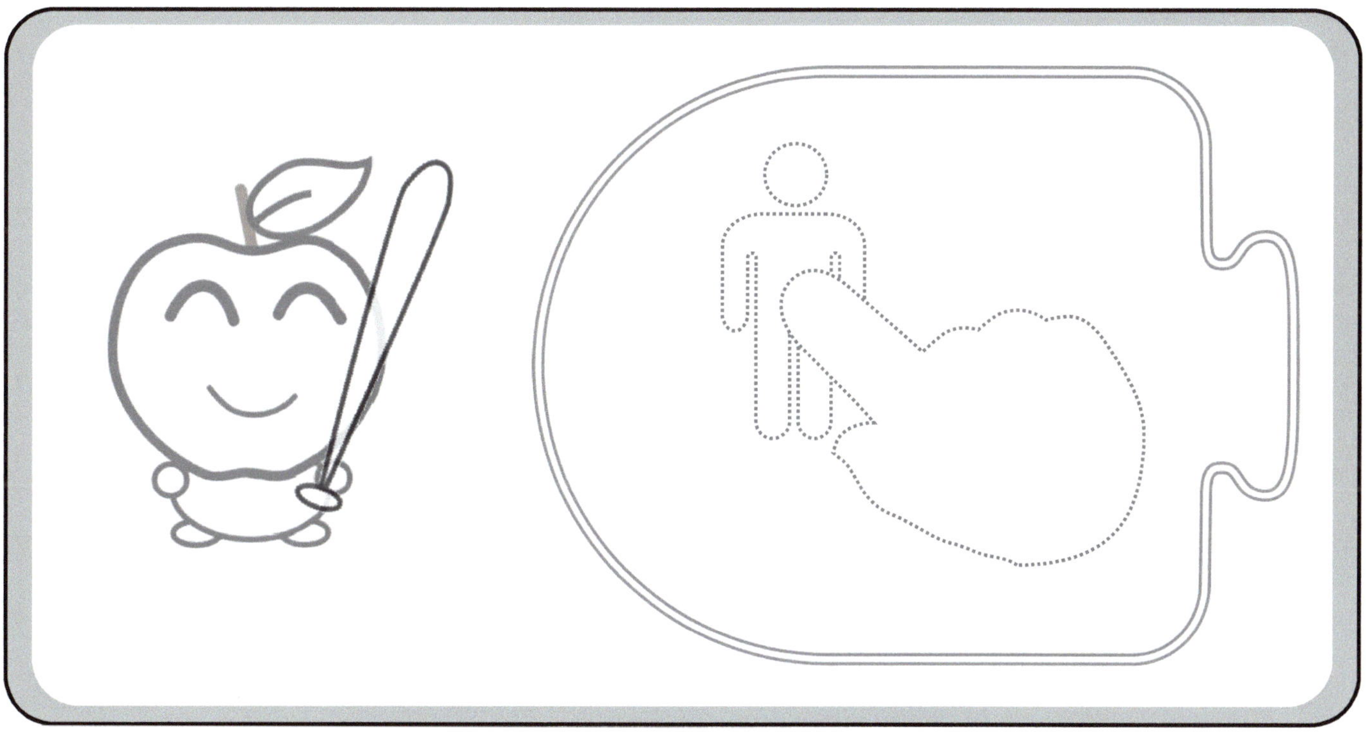

UNIT 6: Track and Field

1.

runner

2.

hurdles

3.

track

Track and Field Chant

Runner, run, run, around the **track**,
jump, jump, jump, over the **hurdles** fast,
race, race, race, try not to come in last,
cross the finish line, do your best!

WORDBANK	
runner	run
hurdles	jump
track	race

UNIT 6: Track and Field

1.

Yes I did it!

2.

Yes I did it!

3.

Yes I did it!

Extra Programming

Add and color runners

Yes I did it!

UNIT 6: Track and Field

Connect:

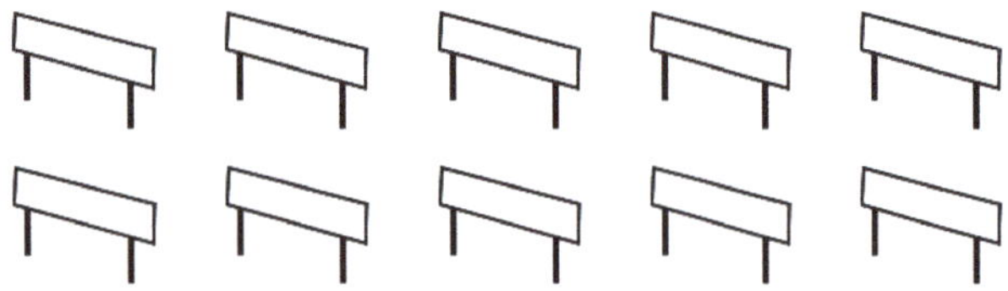

2
8
10

Maze:

UNIT 6: Track and Field

Code Search:

Color:

UNIT 7: Golf

1.

golf ball

2.

golf club

3.

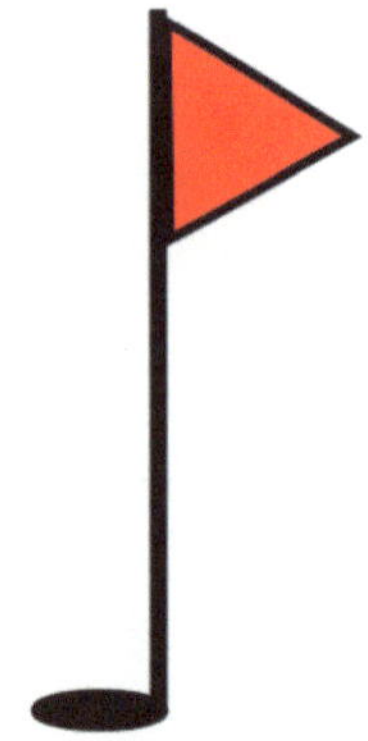

hole

Golf Chant

Shhhh quiet,

look at the **golf ball**, **swing** the **golf club**,

watch it fly high above, land on the green,

and **sink** it in the **hole**

WORDBANK	
golf ball	look
golf club	swing
hole	sink

UNIT 7: Golf

1.

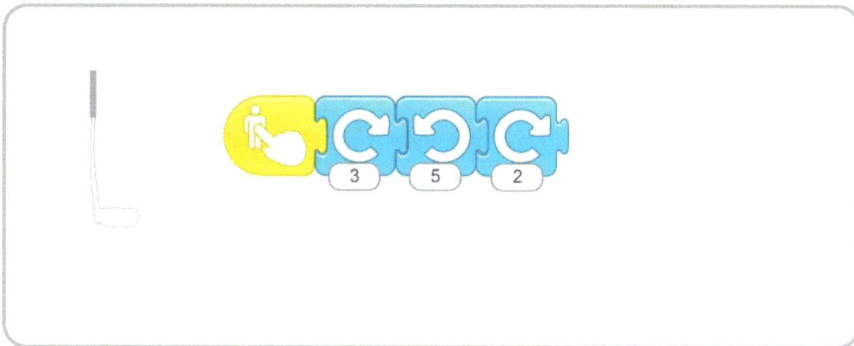

Yes I did it!

2.

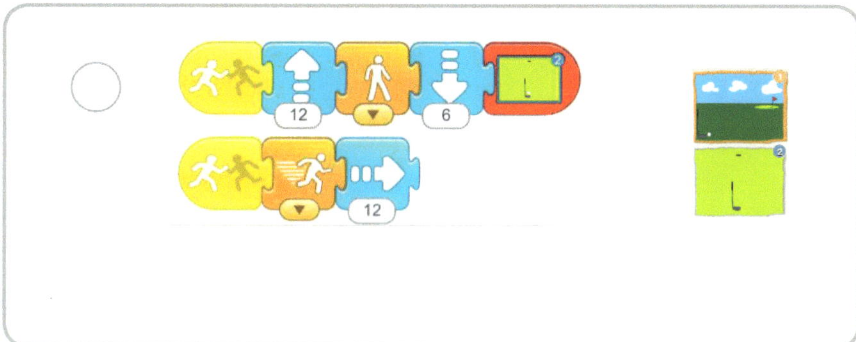

Yes I did it!

3.

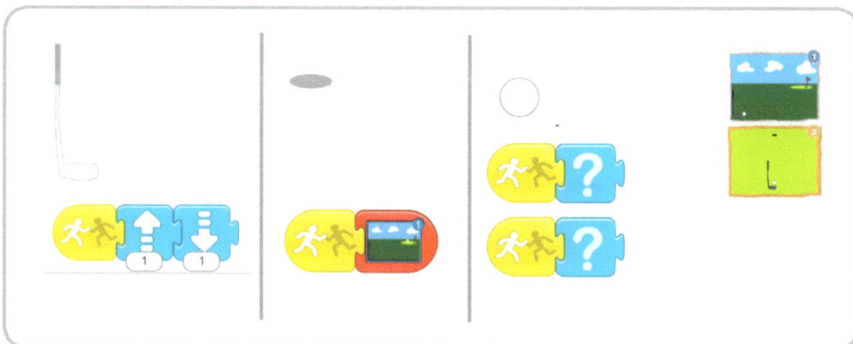

Yes I did it!

Extra Programming

Try moving the hole

Yes I did it!

UNIT 7: Golf

Connect:

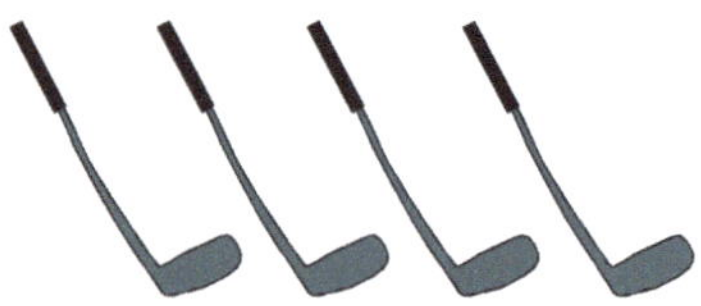

- 4
- 8
- 12

Color and Complete:

Sink the golf ball

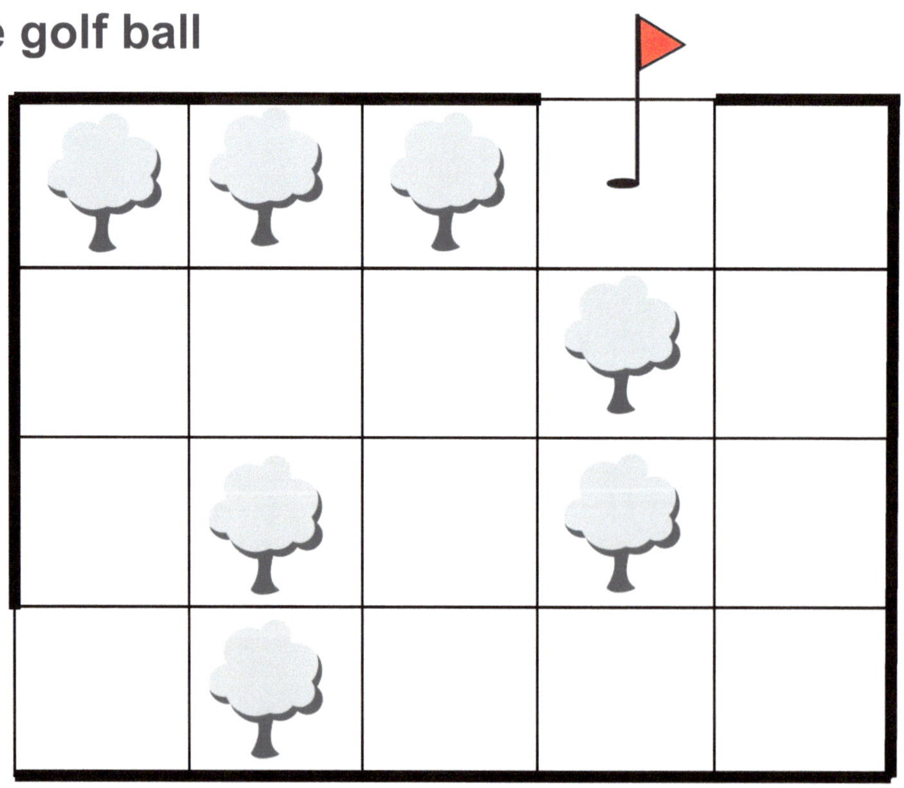

UNIT 7: Golf

Write:

6 6 6

7 7 7

8 8 8

9 9 9

10 10 10

Color:

UNIT 8: Table Tennis

1. 

paddle

2. 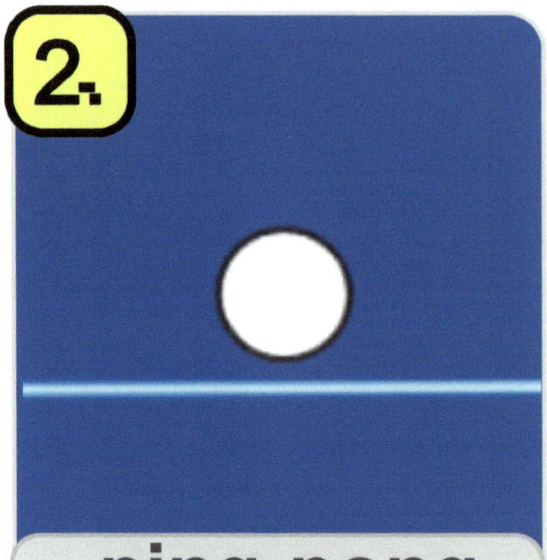

ping-pong ball

3. 

table

Table Tennis Chant

Ping pong **rally**, ping pong **rally**,
serve the **ping-pong ball** with the **paddle**
playing **table** tennis is such a blast,
fall-off the **table**, game set match!

WORDBANK	
paddle	rally
ping-pong ball	serve
table	fall-off

UNIT 8: Table Tennis

1.

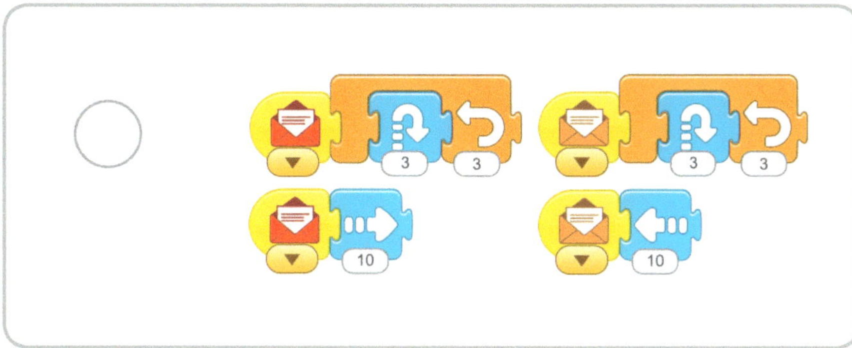

Yes I did it!

2.

Yes I did it!

3.

Yes I did it!

Extra Programming

Yes I did it!

UNIT 8: Table Tennis

Connect:

3

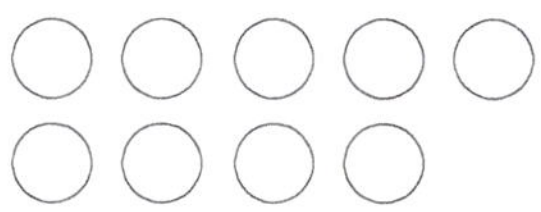

6

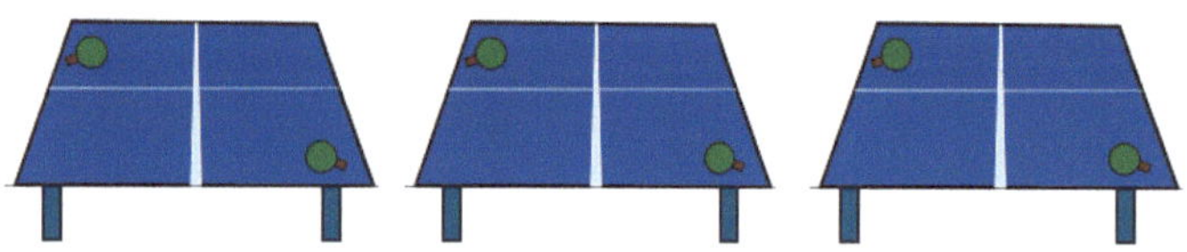

9

Count: 1 - 10

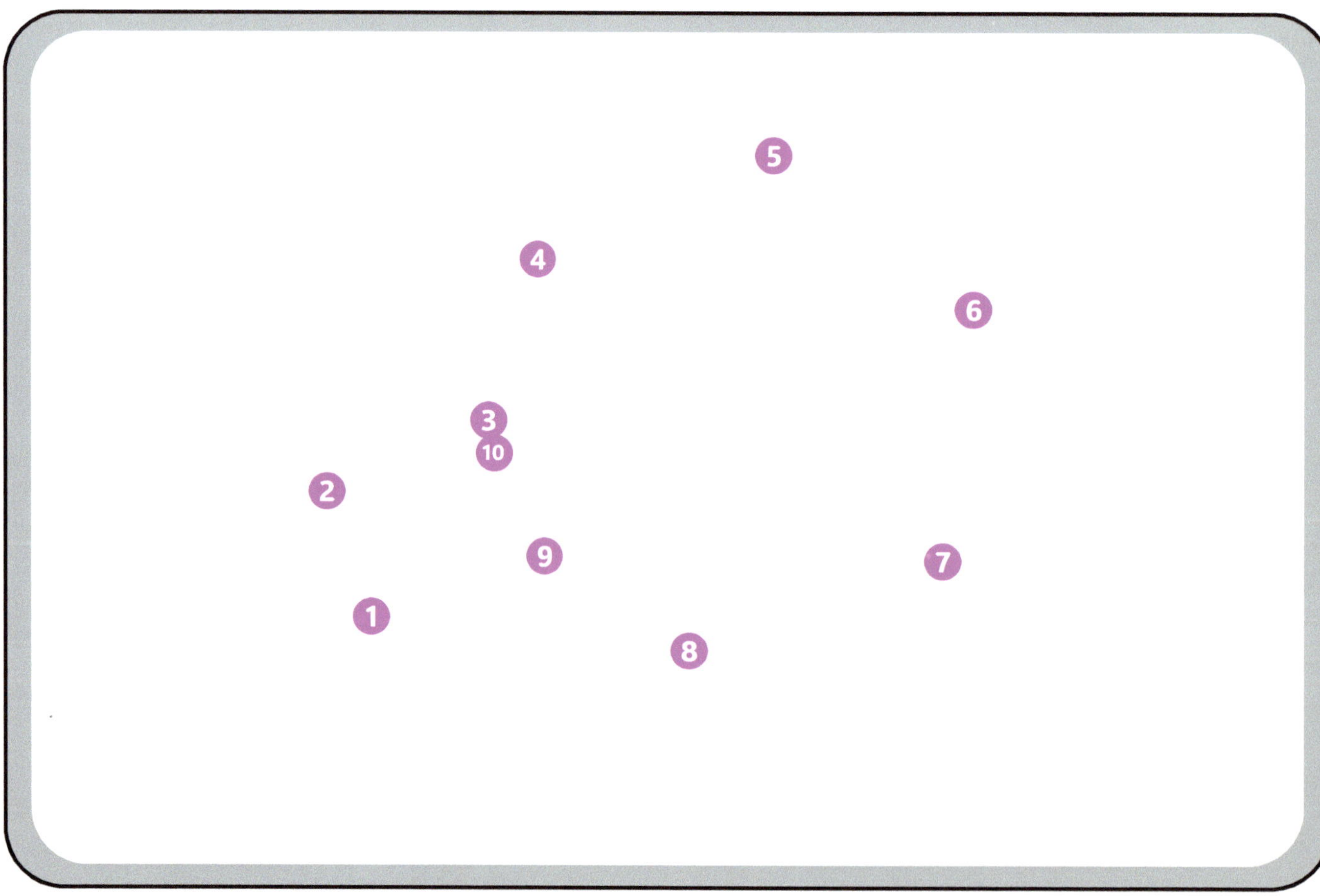

UNIT 8: Table Tennis

Maze:

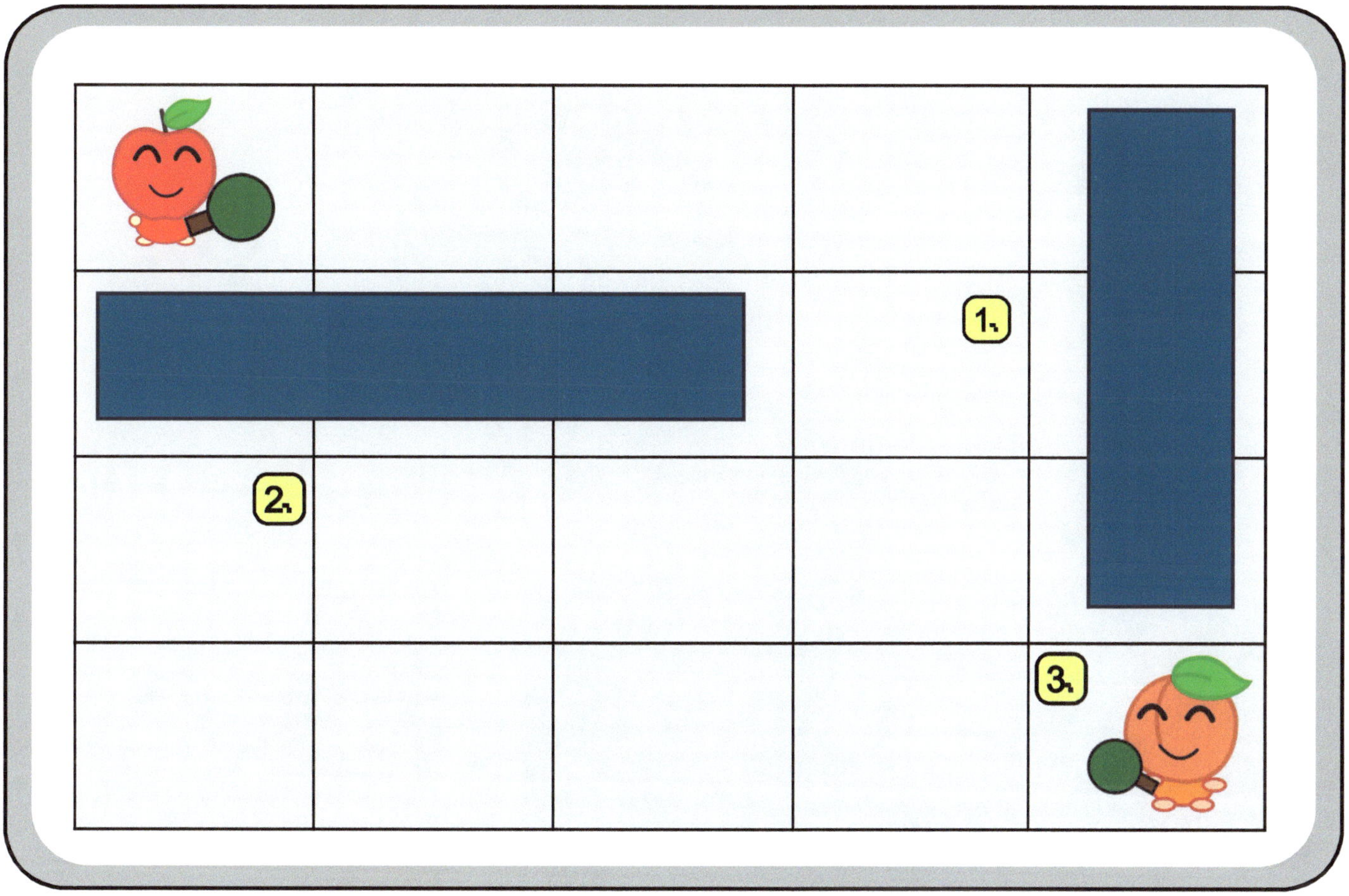

Maze code:

1.

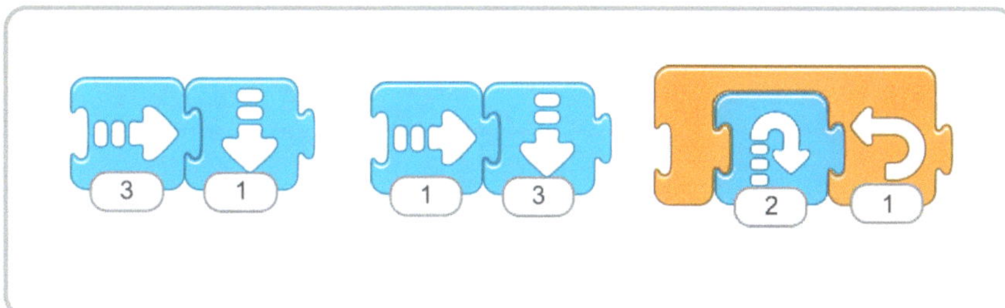

2.

3.

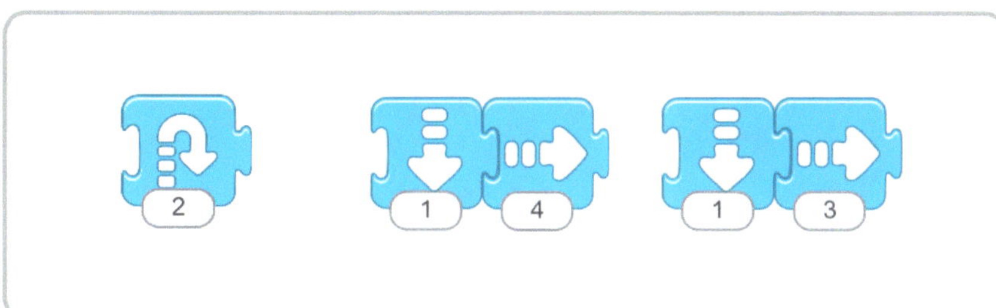

UNIT 9: Tree Design

1.

Christmas tree

2.

present

3.

cookie

Christmas Tree Chant

Make your **Christmas tree**, and
color it beautifully, then Santa he will
leave some **presents**,
and he will **eat** all the **cookies**!

Have you seen Santa?

WORDBANK	
Christmas tree	make
presents	leave
cookies	eat

UNIT 9: Tree Design

1.

Yes I did it!

2.

Yes I did it!

3.

Yes I did it!

Extra Programming

Yes I did it!

Color the cookies

UNIT 9: Tree Design

Connect:

5

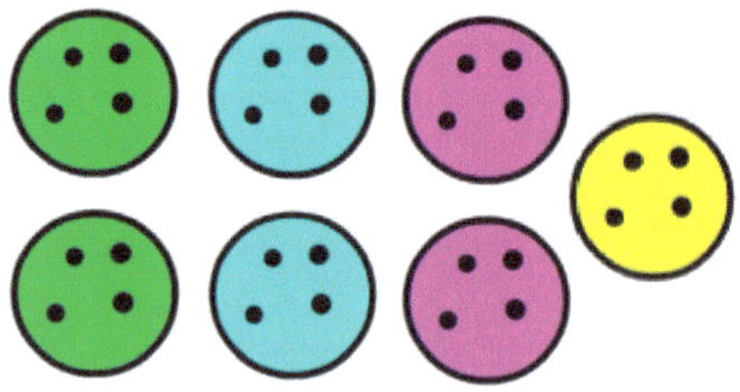

11

7

Draw:

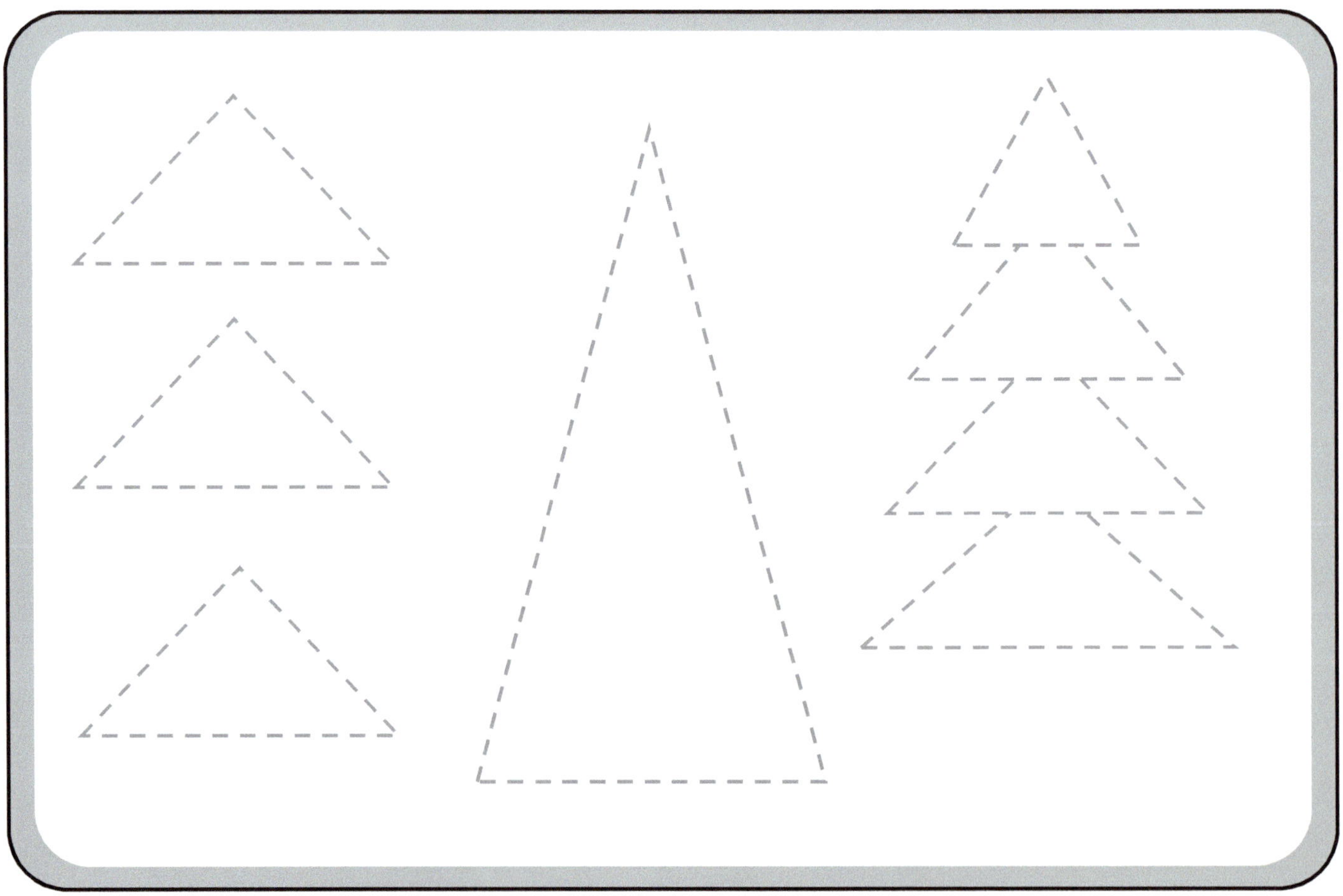

UNIT 9: Tree Design

Circle:

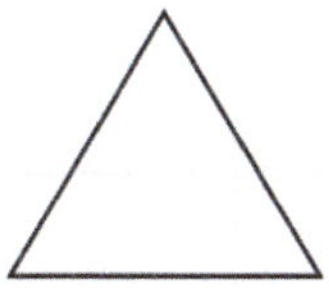

 or 

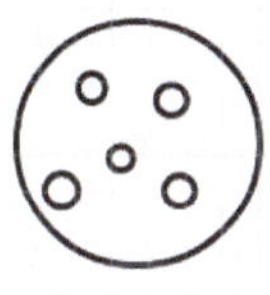

 or 

 or 

Draw:

UNIT 10: Alien Attack

1. aliens

2. moon

3. laser

Alien Chant

Aliens on the **moon**,
aliens walking on the **moon**,
my **laser** gun shoots, attack!
shoot, shoot, shoot, bye bye UFO

WORDBANK	
alien	attack
moon	walking
laser	shoot

UNIT 10: Alien Attack

1.

Yes I did it!

2.

Yes I did it!

3.

Yes I did it!

Extra Programming

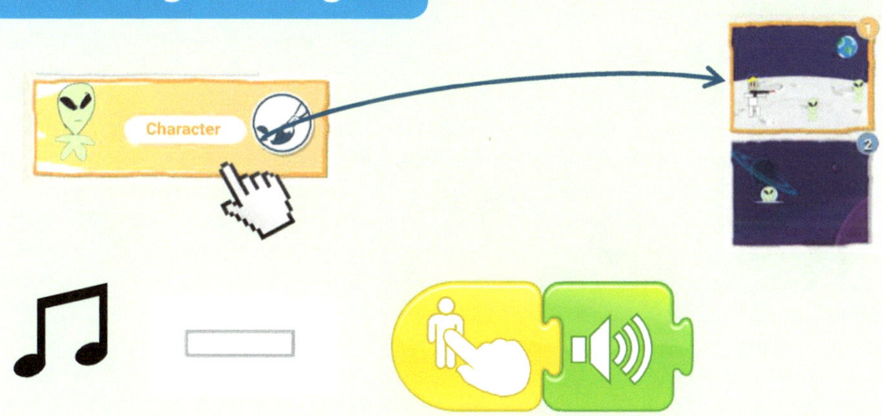

Yes I did it!

UNIT 10: Alien Attack

Connect:

7

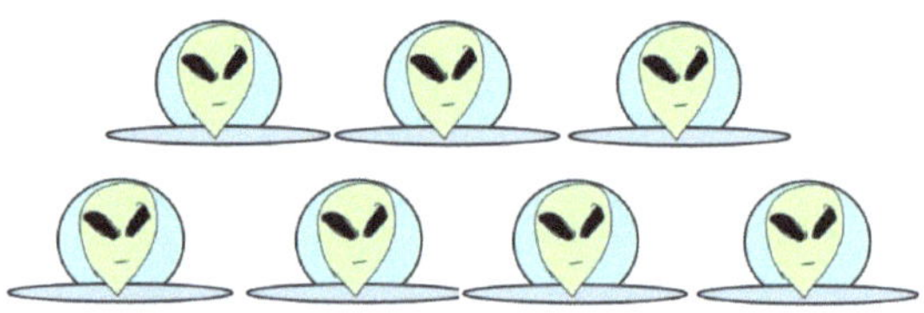

9

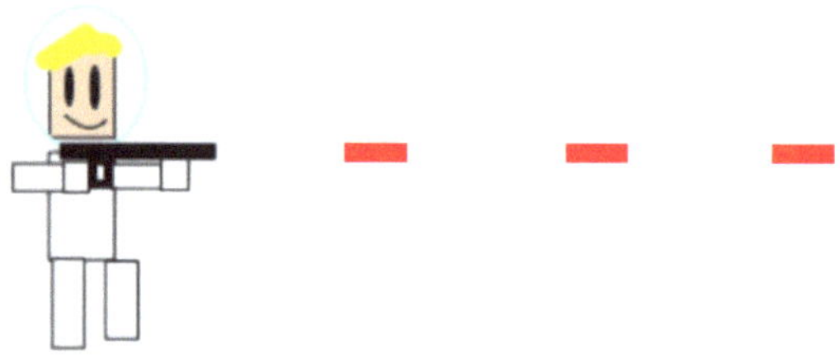

3

Find the Code:

UNIT 10: Alien Attack

Code Search:

Draw:

Start on green flag

Start on tap

Start on bump

Start on message

Send a message

Move forward

Move back

Move up

Move down

Turn right

Turn left

End

Repeat forever

Go to page

Hop

Go home

Say

Grow

Shrink

Reset size

Hide

Show

Play

Wait

Stop

Set speed

repeat

CHESTNUT TREE
LEARNING©

Written by: Kensho Koyama & Mindaugas Ramanauskis

www.ingramcontent.com/pod-product-compliance
Lightning Source LLC
Chambersburg PA
CBHW041324210926
51847CB00003B/44
* 9 7 8 4 9 9 1 4 4 3 1 1 4 *